Zits®

SUPERSIZED

Zits®
SUPERSIZED

A ZITS® TREASURY

by JERRY SCOTT and JIMBORGMAN™

Andrews McMeel
Publishing, LLC

Kansas City

Contains the Director's Cut of GOOD NIGHT DUDE

Zits® is syndicated internationally by King Features Syndicate, Inc. For information, write King Features Syndicate, Inc., 300 West Fifty-Seventh Street, New York, New York 10019.

Zits®: Supersized copyright © 2003 by Zits Partnership. All rights reserved. Printed in China. No part of this book may be used or reproduced in any manner whatsoever without written permission except in the case of reprints in the context of reviews. For information, write Andrews McMeel Publishing,LLC, an Andrews McMeel Universal company, 4520 Main Street, Kansas City, Missouri 64111.

08 09 10 TEN 8 7 6 5

ISBN-13: 978-0-7407-3307-9
ISBN-10: 0-7407-3307-9

Library of Congress Control Number: 2002113775

www.andrewsmcmeel.com

Zits® may be viewed online at:
www.kingfeatures.com

────── **ATTENTION: SCHOOLS AND BUSINESSES** ──────

Andrews McMeel books are available at quantity discounts with bulk purchase for educational, business, or sales promotional use. For information, please write to: Special Sales Department, Andrews McMeel Publishing, LLC,4520 Main Street, Kansas City, Missouri 64111.

Also by Jerry Scott and Jim Borgman

Zits: Sketchbook 1
Growth Spurt: Zits Sketchbook 2
Don't Roll Your Eyes at Me, Young Man!: Sketchbook 3
Are We an "Us"?: Sketchbook 4
Zits Unzipped: Sketchbook 5
Busted!: Sketchbook 6

Humongous Zits
Big Honkin' Zits

To Bob Murphy, for lighting the fuse.

—J.S.

For Suzanne, because it was meant to be.

—J.B.

In the great teen room
There was a telephone
And a stack of tunes
And a picture of—

A girl with some big bazooms

And there were three underwears hanging on chairs

And a comb and a brush and a note from a crush

And a nagging old lady whispering "brush"

Goodnight moon
Goodnight crumbs from my macaroon

Goodnight guitar
Goodnight strings
Goodnight half-eaten bucket of
chicken wings

Goodnight feet
Goodnight toes
Goodnight heaps of dirty clothes

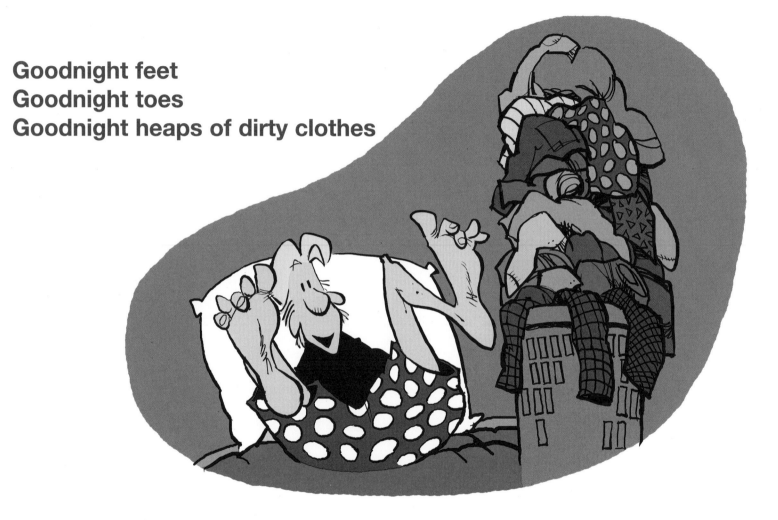

Goodnight modem
Goodnight screen
Goodnight Web sites still unseen

Goodnight clutter
Goodnight dust
Goodnight week-old pizza crust

25

29

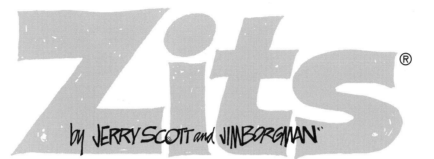

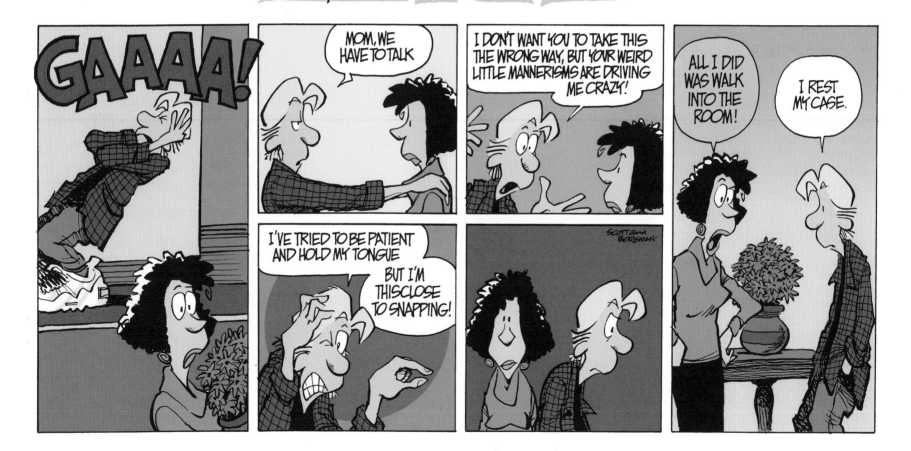

33

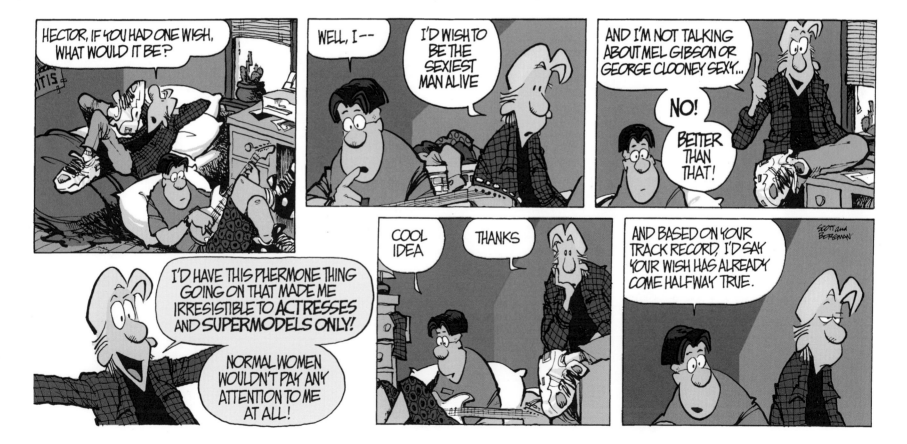

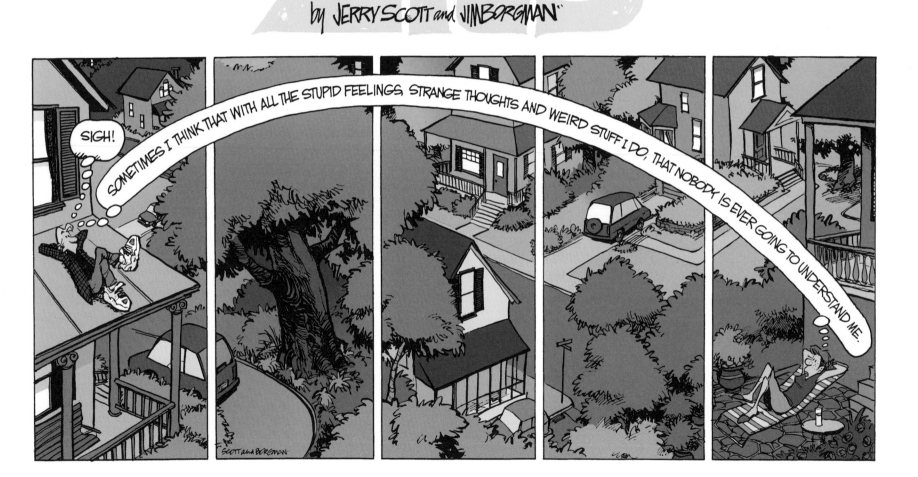

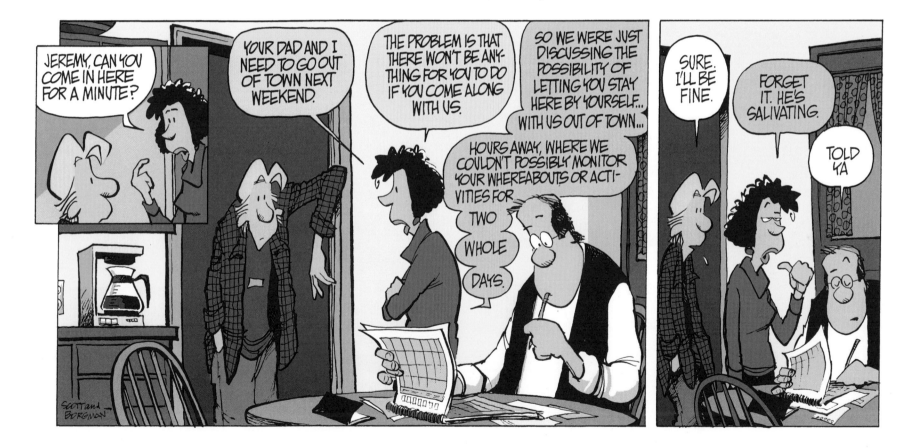

by JERRY SCOTT and JIM BORGMAN

45

49

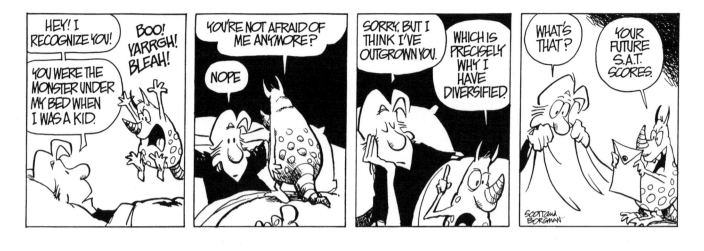

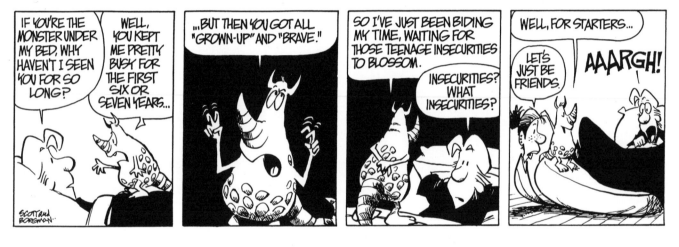

59

61

74

77

82

85

90

95

97

98

100

109

113

114

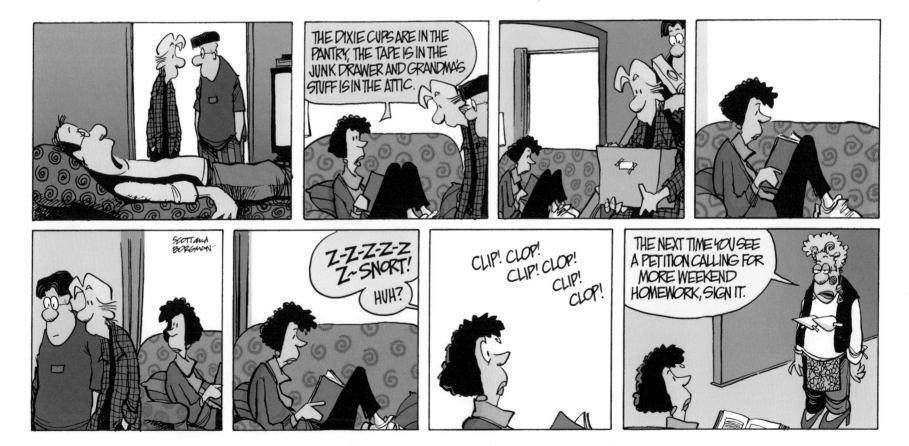

121

124

127

128

131

Zits®

by Jerry Scott and Jim Borgman

139

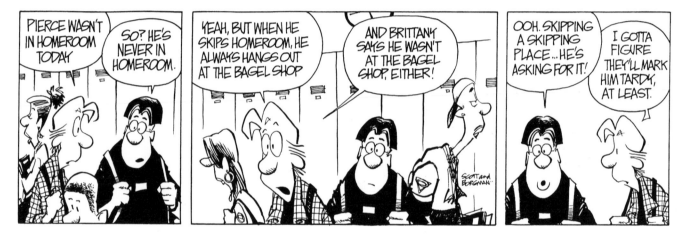

142

143

146

151

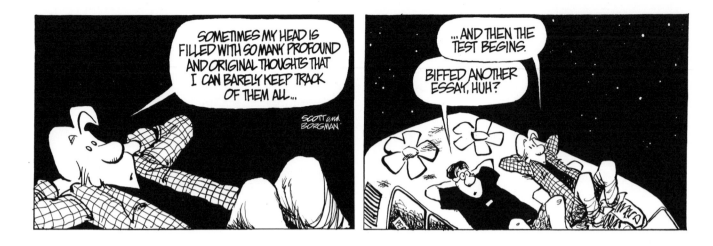

159

163

166

167

169

170

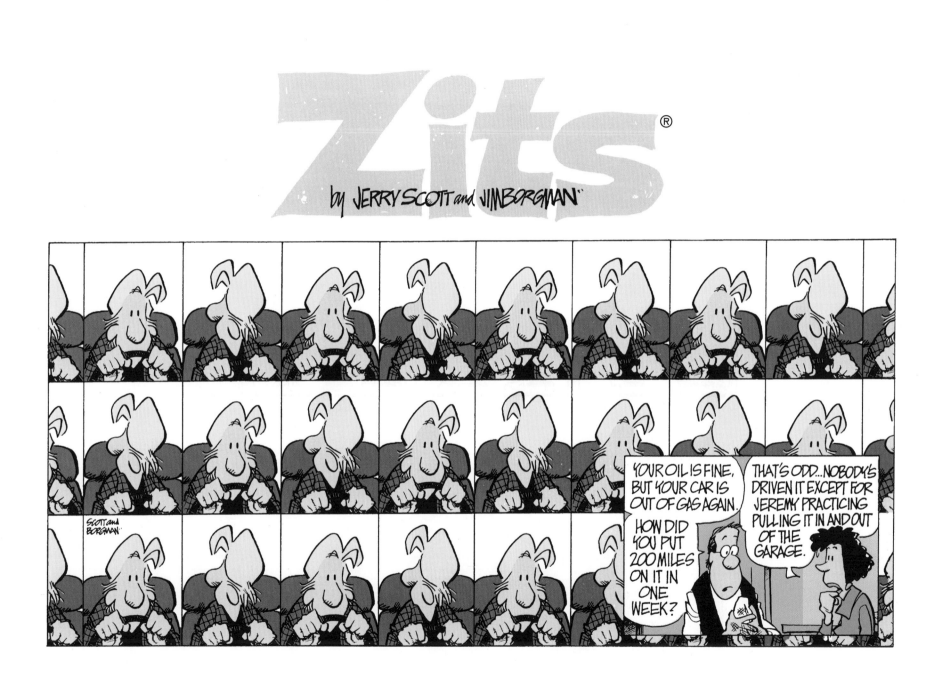

174

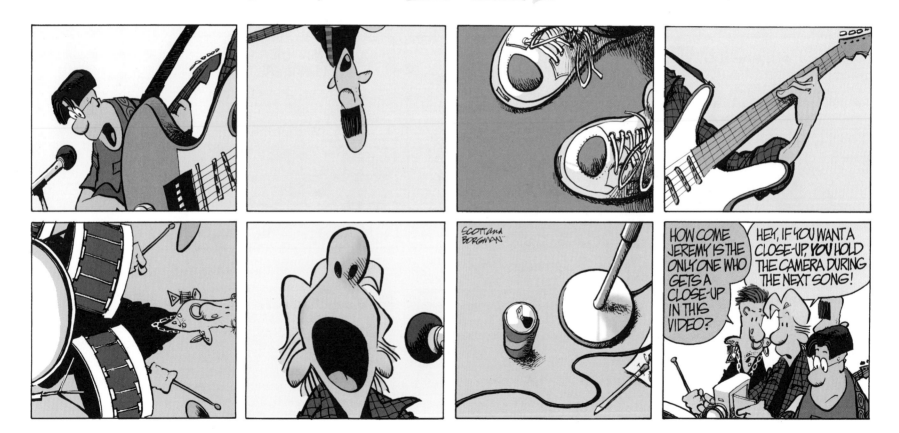

188

189

190

by JERRY SCOTT and JIM BORGMAN

193

195

199

205

207

213

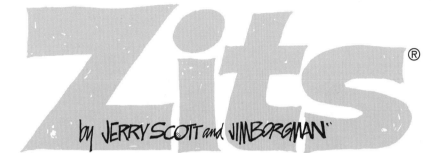

217

219

POP TARTS... LES PAUL... VW VANS... HIGH-FRUCTOSE CORN SYRUP-BASED CARBONATED BEVERAGES...

...HOME-MADE NOODLES... INSTANT MESSENGER... THE WAY GIRLS' HAIR SMELLS RIGHT AFTER THEY WASH IT... ORANGE PEZ...

AHEM!

...OH YEAH. AND THANKS FOR LIFE AND STUFF, TOO.

AMEN!

YELLO?

GOOD EVENING, MR. DUNCAN. THIS IS MITCH FROM ERSATZ COMMUNICATIONS.

DO YOU MAKE THE DECISIONS ABOUT LONG DISTANCE SERVICE IN YOUR HOME?

WELL, SURE. I GUESS.

IT DEPENDS ON WHAT YOU MEAN BY "DECISIONS."

I MEAN, I'M NOT A DICTATOR OR ANYTHING.

I DON'T KNOW... IT'S HARD TO SAY...

MR. DUNCAN, LET ME TALK TO YOUR WIFE.

HANG ON

CUT THE SMOKE AND MIRRORS... WHAT IS THE MOVIE RATED?

MOM, MOM, MOM. WHAT'S IN A LETTER, REALLY?

237

241

244

247

250

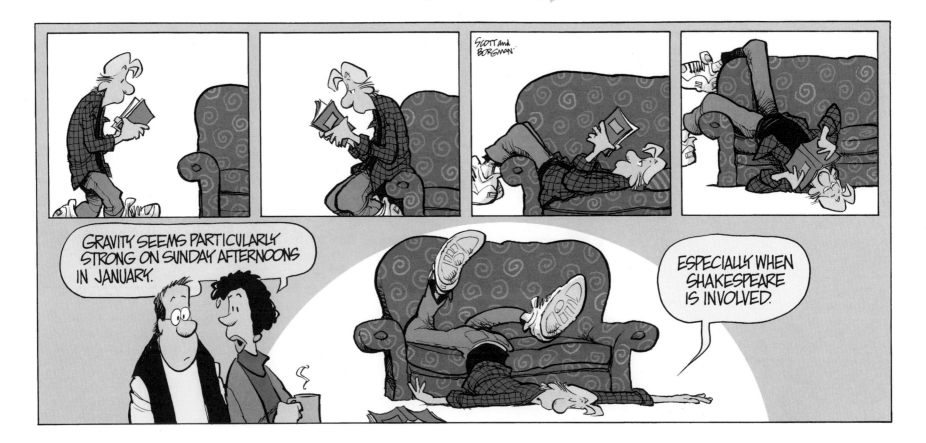

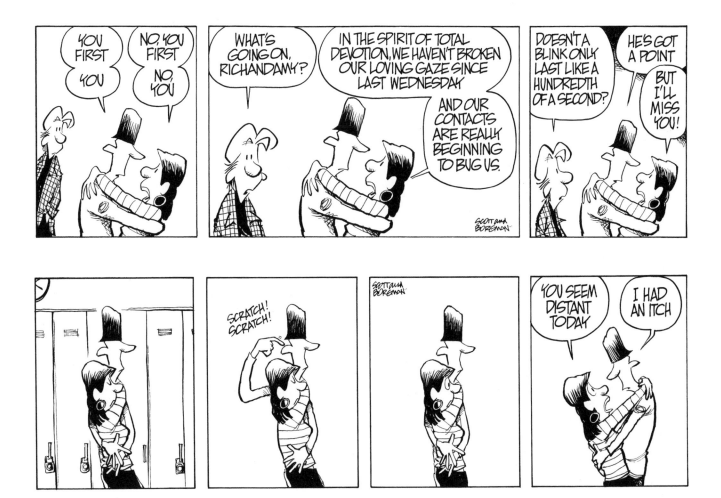

259